NATURE DETECTIVE

British Birds

Victoria Munson

WAYLAND

Published in paperback in 2014 by Wayland
Copyright © Wayland 2014

Wayland
338 Euston Road
London NW1 3BH

Wayland Australia
Level 17/207 KentStreet
Sydney, NSW 2000

Designer: Elaine Wilkinson

Picture acknowledgements:
Shutterstock: Gertjan Hooijer 2(l); Martin Fowler
2(r); Miles Away Photography 3(bl); IbajaUsap
4(br); Bogdan Boev 4(t); Wolfgang Kruck 5 (l);
Vitaly Ilyasov 5(r); Rob Kemp 6; IbajaUsap 7(t);
craigbirdphotos 8(b); Rob Kemp 8(t); Peter Zijlstra
9; Sergey Uryadnikov 10, Valentyn Volkov (whole
apple), panbazil (sliced apple); Bogdan Boev
11(b); IbajaUsap 12; IbajaUsap 13; IbajaUsap
14; Gertjan Hooijer 15; Wolfgang Kruck 16(t);
Borislav Borisov 16(b); Sue Robinson 17(t); S.
Cooper Digital 17(b); Grant Glendinning 18 (t)
Bjorn Stefanson (main); Vitaly Ilyasov 19; Nigel
Dowsett 20(t); SW_Stock 20(b); chris2766 21(t);
Txanbelin 21(b); Rob Kemp 22; Martin Fowler
23(t); Martin Spurny 23(b); Ainars Aunins 24(t);
Anatoliy Lukich 24(b); Gucio_25 (t); xpixel 25(b);
Borislav Borisov 26(t); IbajaUsap 26(b); Larsek
27; Menno Schaefer 28; Mircea Bezergheanu 29;
Miles Away Photography 30; S. Cooper Digital 31;
Rob Kemp 32; Eric Isselee 33(t); SW_Stock 33(b);
Menno Schaefer 34; Rick Wylie 35; Verevkin 36;
Martin Fowler 37; RazvanZinica 41 (b); Becky
Stares 44 (t); Jerome Whittingham 56 (t), godrick
56(b); John Braid 57; wim claes 58 (t) Sebastian
Knight 58 (m), Peter Zijlstra 58 (b); Menno
Schaefer 62; Borislav Borisov 63; John Braid 64;
iStock Photo: Andrew Howe 3(tl), 11 (tr); rekemp
3(tr); Christian Musat 3(br); Leopardinatree 4(bl);
Roberto Zocchi 7(b); Andrew Howe 11(t); Karel
Broz 38; Borislav Borisov 39; Vassiliy Vishnevskiy
40; Anette Andersen 41(t); thawats 42(t); Andrew
Howe 42(b); Andrew Howe 43; David Fowler 44
(b); Christopher Smith 45; Derek Audette 46; Iliuta
Goean 47; Britta Kasholm-Tengve 48; Christian
Musat 49; Roberto Zocchi 50; Roger Whiteway
51(t), shurub (b); Maurizio Bonora 52; rekemp
53; Liz Leyden 54(t); Uwe Ohse 54(b); Roger
Whiteway 55. Artwork 59: Peter Bull

A cataloguing record for this title is available at the
British Library. Dewey number: 598'.0941
ISBN: 978 0 7502 8341 0

Printed in China
10 9 8 7 6 5 4 3 2 1

Wayland is a division of Hachette Children's Books,
an Hachette UK company
www.hachette.co.uk

Contents

Be a nature detective!

To be a nature detective, you need to be observant, patient and quiet. Birds scare easily and can be shy, so it might take time before you can spot one. Listen carefully. Sometimes you can hear birds before you see them.

Where to see birds

You can watch birds from your window or go on a nature walk through woodland, along a river or by the sea. There are different types of bird in each habitat.

You could ask to visit a different habitat at the weekend or for a school trip. If you're going out to look for birds, you may need to wear wellies and a waterproof jacket. Take binoculars and a notebook and pens.

Jay

Coot

Mistle Thrush

Pied Wagtail

Greenfinch

Making notes

Once you've spotted a bird you don't know the name of, use a notebook to write down and sketch some details about the birds. That way, if the bird flies off you can refer to your notes to help you identify it using this book. Note down its colour, shape, size, where it was and what it was eating. Get to know the different parts of a bird's body (see page 7).

Birdwatcher's code

1 Birds come first. Never disturb or frighten them. Try to keep away from their nests. Remember: it is against the law to take birds' eggs.

2 Protect habitats. Don't drop litter or pull up any plants.

3 Follow the countryside code. Ask permission before you go onto private land. Do not walk on crops or leave gates open.

You can see birds in many different local habitats.

How to identify birds

There are various features you can note down to help you identify birds, such as their size, shape, colour and where you saw them. Once you've written down some notes, try to make a sketch of them.

Size

Get to know some common birds, such as a Robin, Blackbird and Pigeon. Then you can use the size of them to compare to other birds.

Robin

Shape

What shape is the bird? Does it remind you of another bird? In which case, they might belong to the same family group. Search in this book for birds in a similar family. The type of bill they have might also give you a clue as to which group of birds they belong to.

Bills

Tits: small bill for getting insects and seeds
Blackbird: bigger bill for worms and fruit
Mallard: duck bill for shovelling up plants, weeds and insects
Bird of prey: hooked bill for catching and eating small mammals and birds

Feet

Feet are also a clue: if a bird has talons, it is usually a bird of prey because they need sharp talons for catching animals. If they have webbed feet, the bird can probably be found near water.

Blue Tit

Colour

What colour are the bird's upperparts, underparts, head and tail? Make a note of any prominent patches of colour, such as a red crown or a white rump. Does it have any other obvious markings, such as stripes, streaks or bars? Remember that males and females are often different colours, and that some birds, such as the Great Crested Grebe, change colour between summer and winter. Some species of young are also a different colour from the adults until they are fully grown birds.

Habitat

Make a note of where you were when you saw the bird. Were you on a woodland walk, in a park, or looking out into your garden? Some familiar birds, such as Blackbirds, finches and Robins, live in many different habitats, whereas some species, such as ducks and swans, are usually only found by water.

Saturday 8th February

Woodland walk (2.50pm)

Tufts

Dark brown wing

Short bill

Pale brown chest

Male and female Mallard

7

Field guide

House Sparrow

Size: 14–15 cm
Latin name: *Passer domesticus*
Family: Sparrows
Habitat: Towns and cities, farms
Food: Seeds, scraps and insects
Life span: 2–5 years

The House Sparrow is one of the most familiar small birds in Britain. The male has a grey crown, underside and rump, and a black bib. Its brown back is streaked with black and it has a white bar on its wings. The female House Sparrow is much plainer than the male, without the black markings.

Robin

Size: 14 cm
Latin name: *Erithacus rubecula*
Family: Chats and thrushes
Habitat: Parks, gardens, woodland and hedgerows
Food: Worms, seeds, fruit and insects
Life span: 3–5 years

Robins are easily recognised by their orange-red breast, brown back and rounded shape. Males and females look alike. Their young have a dark brown, speckled plumage. Robins sing all year round.

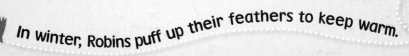

In winter, Robins puff up their feathers to keep warm.

Starling

Size: 21 cm
Latin name: *Sturnus vulgaris*
Family: Starlings
Habitat: Towns and cities, farms
Food: Insects and fruit
Life span: Up to 5 years

Purple-green sheen on wing

Short tail

Starlings mimic the sounds of other birds, mammals and even telephones and car alarms!

They are one of Britain's most common garden birds. A Starling looks black from a distance, but up close it has a green or purple sheen on its wing. Starlings live in large flocks and can be very noisy when grouped together.

Blackbird

Size: 25 cm
Latin name: *Turdus merula*
Family: Thrushes
Habitat: Gardens and woodland
Food: Insects, fruit and berries
Life span: Up to 5 years

Bright orange beak

Male Blackbirds are black with
a bright yellowy beak and yellow rings
around their eyes. Females and their young
are dark brown with a speckled throat. They feed
on worms and can be seen hopping across gardens.
Look out for them singing loudly from on top of a
high perch. The male Blackbird has a beautiful song.
It sings all through the breeding season.

Song Thrush

Size: 22 cm
Latin name: *Turdus philomelos*
Family: Thrushes
Habitat: Parks, gardens, woodland and hedgerows
Food: Worms, slugs, insects, fruit and berries
Life span: Up to 5 years

The Song Thrush is pale brown with a cream-coloured breast flecked with dark-brown spots. It is slightly smaller than a Blackbird. When it is in flight, you can see its wings are slightly orange underneath. Its spots are heart-shaped.

Mistle Thrush

Size: 27 cm
Latin name: *Turdus viscivorus*
Family: Thrushes
Habitat: Parks, gardens, woodland and hedgerows
Food: Worms, slugs, insects, fruit and berries
Life span: 5–10 years

The Mistle Thrush is bigger than both the Song Thrush and the Blackbird. You can tell the two thrushes apart because Mistle Thrushes are bigger and they do not have the orange colouring beneath their wings. Their spots are wider and more defined than a Song Thrush's.

Watch for flocks in July and August.

Great Tit

Size: 14 cm
Latin name: *Parus major*
Family: Tits
Habitat: Gardens, woodland and fields
Food: Insects, seeds and nuts
Life span: 2–3 years

Great Tits have a clutch of 5–11 eggs in April or May.

The Great Tit is the largest member of the tit family. It has a distinctive black stripe down its yellow breast and a glossy black head. Great Tits are common visitors to bird tables and garden feeders.

Blue cap

Blue Tit

Size: 11.5 cm
Latin name: *Cyanistes caeruleus*
Family: Tits
Habitat: Gardens, parks and woodland
Food: Insects, caterpillars, seeds and nuts
Life span: 2–3 years

Yellow breast

Blue Tits are very
colourful, lively birds.
They have a yellow breast
with blue wings and a blue cap.
A pair of Blue Tits can collect hundreds
of caterpillars each day to feed their young.
By the time Blue Tit chicks fly the nest, they
may have eaten up to 10,000 caterpillars.

Coal Tit

Size: 11.5 cm
Latin name: *Periparus ater*
Family: Tits
Habitat: Parks, gardens and woodland
Food: Insects, seeds and nuts
Life span: 2–3 years

Short tail

The Coal Tit has a
black crown and bib,
white cheeks, and a grey belly.
It also has a white patch on the back of
its head. The Coal Tit usually nests close to
the ground, or even underground, at the base
of a tree. It also likes to nest in old stone walls.

Long-tailed Tit

Size: 14 cm
Latin name: *Aegithalos caudatus*
Family: Tits
Habitat: Woodland, parks and gardens
Food: Insects and seeds
Life span: 2–3 years

Pale pink
chest

Long tail

Easily identifiable by its
long tail, both males and
females are black, white and pale
pink with white crowns. The tail is longer
than its body. They can mostly be seen in
woods, bushes and in hedgerows, where they
form small flocks of about 20 birds.

Pied Wagtail

Size: 18 cm
Latin name: *Motacilla alba*
Family: Pipits and wagtails
Habitat: Fields, parks and towns
Food: Insects
Life span: Up to 5 years

Pied Wagtails are distinctive black and white birds with long tails which they 'wag' up and down. They have a black bib and crown with a white face and belly. The male is darker than the female.

Grey Wagtail

Size: 18–19 cm
Latin name: *Motacilla cinerea*
Family: Pipits and wagtails
Habitat: Fields, farmland, rivers
Food: Insects
Life span: Up to 5 years

Yellow rump

Grey Wagtails have a grey back and wings, but a distinctive yellow breast and rump. Their tail is longer than the Pied Wagtail's.

Look for Grey Wagtails near rivers, streams and ponds.

Cocked tail

Wren

Size: 9–10 cm
Latin name: *Troglodytes troglodytes*
Family: Wrens
Habitat: Woodland, farmland and heathland
Food: Insects and spiders
Life span: 2–5 years

The Wren is a tiny brown bird with an upright tail found near the ground in thickets or brambles. For such a small bird, the Wren has a very loud voice.

Black streaks

Dunnock

Size: 14.5 cm
Latin name: *Prunella modularis*
Family: Accentors
Habitat: Woodland, edges of farmland, parks and gardens
Food: Insects, spiders, seeds and nuts
Life span: Up to 5 years

The Dunnock is a brown and grey bird with a slender black beak. Dunnocks can be hard to spot because they like to creep around in bushes, looking for insects and worms to eat. When two rival males meet though there is a lot of wing-flicking and loud calling. Males and females look alike.

Chaffinch

Size: 15 cm
Latin name: *Fringilla coelebs*
Family: Finches
Habitat: Parks, gardens, woodland and hedgerows
Food: Insects and seeds
Life span: 2–5 years

Female Chaffinch

Listen out for Chaffinches singing in early spring.

Male Chaffinch

The male Chaffinch is one of Britain's most colourful birds. Males have a pinky face and breast and a blue-grey crown. Females are sandy brown. Both male and female Chaffinches have black and white wings, and a green rump. During the winter, Chaffinches often group together in large flocks in the open countryside and on the edges of woodland, where they search for seeds to eat.

Greenfinch

Size: 15 cm
Latin name: *Carduelis chloris*
Family: Finches
Habitat: Woodland, parks and gardens
Food: Seeds, berries and insects
Life span: 2–3 years

Yellow on wing

The Greenfinch is a popular garden visitor. The male Greenfinch's plumage is mostly yellow and green with bits of grey. Its forked tail has a dark tip. Females can get confused for sparrows, but when they fly off you'll see a flicker of yellow in their tail and wings. The female Greenfinch also has yellow patches on its wings.

Goldfinch

Size: 12–13 cm
Latin name: *Carduelis carduelis*
Family: Finches
Habitat: Gardens, parks and countryside
Food: Plants, seeds and insects
Life span: 2–3 years

Goldfinches, as their name suggests, are golden-coloured finches. They have white bars on their wings and a black, white and red face. In autumn, they gather in large flocks. Goldfinches decorate their nests with flowers.

Bullfinch

Size: 15–16 cm
Latin name: *Pyrrhula pyrrhula*
Family: Finches
Habitat: Woodland and hedgerows
Food: Seeds, buds and insects
Life span: 2–3 years

Black crown

The male Bullfinch has a bright red chest while the female has a yellow chest, almost like a Goldfinch. Both sexes have a black cap and tail. They are shy birds, and therefore difficult to spot.

Black crown

Siskin

Size: 12 cm
Latin name: *Carduelis spinus*
Family: Finches
Habitat: Woodland
Food: Seeds and insects
Life span: 2–3 years

Siskins are bright yellow with black bars on their wings. The male (above) has a black crown. In spring, they can be seen in gardens when seeds and insects are scarce.

Blackcap

Size: 13 cm
Latin name: *Sylvia atricapilla*
Family: Warblers
Habitat: Woodland, parks and gardens
Food: Insects and berries
Life span: Up to 5 years

Male Blackcaps have a glossy black cap, while females (pictured) have a chestnut one. They both have pale-brown bodies and light-brown wings. They come to Britain from Europe in the spring and stay until the autumn.

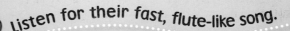

Listen for their fast, flute-like song.

Collared Dove

Size: 31–33 cm
Latin name: *Streptopelia decaocto*
Family: Pigeons and doves
Habitat: Gardens, parks and farmland
Food: Seeds and grain
Life span: Up to 10 years

Black collar

Collared Doves
are recognisable
because of the black 'collar' on
their neck and their pinkish plumage.
They have deep red eyes and reddish feet.
Listen for their 'coo-COO-coo' call.

White patch

Woodpigeon

Size: 41 cm
Latin name: *Columba palumbus*
Family: Pigeons and doves
Habitat: Fields, woodland, parks and gardens
Food: Crops, buds, shoots, berries, seeds and nuts.
Life span: Up to 10 years

Woodpigeons are the largest and most common of our pigeons. They are grey and have white bars on their wings, which are easier to see when the pigeon is flying. They also have white patches on the sides of their neck. In winter, they can often be found in huge flocks.

Green neck

Feral Pigeon

Size: 32 cm
Latin name: *Columba livia*
Family: Pigeons and doves
Habitat: Fields, woodland, parks and gardens
Food: Seeds and cereals
Life span: Up to 10 years

This common city bird comes in many different shades, from black to white, grey or brown. They usually have a green or purple sheen on their neck and black wing bars.

Carrion Crow

Size: 46 cm
Latin name: *Corvus corone*
Family: Crows
Habitat: Farmland and woodland
Food: Carrion, insects, worms, seeds, fruit and scraps
Life span: 5–10 years

Carrion Crows are usually seen alone or in pairs. They are completely black with a powerful bill. They are intelligent, adaptable and can live almost anywhere. Carrion Crows hop rather than walk.

Raven

Size: 62 cm
Latin name: *Corvus corax*
Family: Crows
Habitat: Farmland and woodland
Food: Carrion, worms and eggs
Life span: 10–15 years

The Raven is a very large bird. It is all black with a large bill, and a shaggy throat. In flight, you can see its diamond-shaped tail. It has a longer neck than other crows.

The Tower of London is guarded by 7 Ravens.

Black cap

Jackdaw

Size: 33–34 cm
Latin name: *Corvus monedula*
Family: Crows
Habitat: Fields, woodland, parks and gardens
Food: Insects, seeds and scraps
Life span: 5–10 years

The Jackdaw is the smallest crow commonly seen in Britain. It looks black all over, but has a grey neck and cheeks. Jackdaws normally live in open countryside. During the winter, Jackdaws often join Rooks to make large flocks. They have a distinctive 'jack jack' call.

Rook

Size: 44–46 cm
Latin name: *Corvus frugilegus*
Family: Crows
Habitat: Farmland and woodland
Food: Worms, grains and insects
Life span: 5–10 years

Rooks are slightly smaller than the Carrion Crow and look like they're wearing 'baggy trousers'. You usually see Rooks in large flocks and they nest in colonies (rookeries) at the top of tall, bare trees.

Magpie

Size: 46 cm
Latin name: *Pica pica*
Family: Crows
Habitat: Fields and gardens
Food: Insects, plants, carrion, small birds and eggs
Life span: 10–15 years

Magpies are as big as crows, but have distinctive black and white plumage. Up close you can see a green gloss on the tail. They are usually seen in pairs but sometimes flock together in groups of 20–40 to nest.

Jay

Size: 34–35 cm
Latin name: *Garrulus glandarius*
Family: Crows
Habitat: Woodland, parks and larger gardens
Food: Acorns, nuts, seeds and insects
Life span: Up to 5 years

This colourful member of the crow family has a pinkish-brown body and blue and black wings. It is as large as a pigeon, with a long tail and a short black bill. They are quite shy, so watch for their white rumps as they fly.

Look out for Jays burying acorns in autumn.

Ring-necked Parakeet

Size: 39–43 cm
Latin name: *Psittacula krameri*
Family: Parrots
Habitat: Parks and gardens
Food: Fruit, berries, nuts and seeds
Life span: 20–30 years

Red hooked
bill

Long
tail

This type of Parakeet
escaped from collections near
London and bred in the wild. They
can now be found across the south-east of
England. They are unmistakable with their green
bodies, long tails and red bills. Parakeets often form
large flocks and can be very noisy!

Great Spotted Woodpecker

Size: 22–23 cm
Latin name: *Dendrocopos major*
Family: Wrynecks and woodpeckers
Habitat: Woodland
Food: Insects, seeds and nuts
Life span: 5–10 years

Great Spotted Woodpeckers strike a branch 40 times a second.

The Great Spotted Woodpecker has striking black and white markings and a bright red patch under its tail. The male also has a red patch on the back of its head. Young birds have a red crown. Like all woodpeckers, the Great Spotted Woodpecker has two toes facing backwards and two toes facing forwards. This means it can cling on to the trunks of trees and drill into the bark with its beak, looking for insects. It has a very distinctive bouncing flight.

Red cap

Green Woodpecker

Size: 30–33 cm
Latin name: *Picus viridis*
Family: Wrynecks and woodpeckers
Habitat: Woodland
Food: Insects, especially ants
Life span: 5–10 years

The Green Woodpecker has a long, sticky tongue.

The Green Woodpecker is the largest of the three woodpeckers that breed in Britain. Green Woodpeckers spend a lot of their time on the ground looking for ants. Males and females are yellow-green with red heads. They have a short tail and a long beak.

Barn Owl

Size: 33–39 cm
Latin name: *Tyto alba*
Family: Owls
Habitat: Countryside
Food: Mice, voles and shrews
Life span: 5–10 years

Speckled
breast

Barn Owls have
snowy-white underparts
and a honey-coloured back and
wings. They have a large head with a
heart-shaped face. Barn Owls hunt mostly
alone at dusk, or sometimes by day, so of
all the owls, this is the one you might catch
a glimpse of. Look out for them perched
on roadside verges.

Tawny Owl

Size: 37–39 cm
Latin name: *Strix aluco*
Family: Owls
Habitat: Woodland
Food: Small mammals and birds, rodents, frogs, fish and insects
Life span: Up to 10 years

Large, round head

Row of white spots

Pale, streaked breast

The Tawny Owl is reddish-brown with paler feathers on its breast. It has a round body and face. By day, it roosts in a tree, and it hunts at night. You are unlikely to see it in daylight unless it has been disturbed. They fly quickly and silently, so they are very tricky to spot.

Pheasant

Size: 53–89 cm
Latin name: *Phasianus colchicus*
Family: Partridges, quails and pheasants
Habitat: Farmland, woodland and hedgerows
Food: Seeds, grain and shoots
Life span: 5–10 years

Pheasants are game birds – people hunt them for food or sport.

Long stiff tail

Male Pheasants have rich golden brown and black markings on the body and tail, a dark green head and red face wattles. Females are paler brown and black and are much smaller.

Grey Partridge

Size: 29–31 cm
Latin name: *Perdix perdix*
Family: Partridges, quails and pheasants
Habitat: Farmland, woodland and hedgerows
Food: Leaves, seeds and insects
Life span: Up to 5 years

This game bird has an orange face, brown bars on its grey wings and mottled grey feathers. It is to be found mainly on the ground (and not in pear trees!). The Grey Partridge lays one of the largest clutches of eggs in the world, 15–19 eggs per nest.

Cuckoo

Size: 30–32 cm
Latin name: *Cuculus canorus*
Family: Cuckoos
Habitat: Woodland and farmland
Food: Insects
Life span: Up to 10 years

The Cuckoo is about the same size as a Collared Dove, with stripey, blue-grey upperparts. Cuckoos come to Britain in late spring. They have pointed wings and a long tail, and are usually found alone.

Cuckoos lay their eggs in other birds' nests.

Grey head

Kestrel

Size: 32–35 cm
Latin name: *Falco tinnunculus*
Family: Falcons
Habitat: Countryside, motorway verges
Food: Small mammals and birds
Life span: Up to 15 years

Kestrels can often be seen perching on posts and telegraph wires.

The Kestrel is a small bird of
prey with a long tail and pointed wings.
The male has a spotted reddish-brown back,
grey head and grey tail. The female is brown with
black markings. Both have a black band at the tip
of their tail. They hunt in the open, hovering above
ground before swooping down on their prey.

Buzzard

Size: 51–57 cm
Latin name: *Buteo buteo*
Family: Hawks, vultures and eagles
Habitat: Fields, woodland and moorland
Food: Small mammals, birds and carrion
Life span: Up to 25 years

Buzzards are now the most common bird of prey in Britain. They have broad, rounded wings and are brownish all over. They can often be seen sat on posts near to the roadside.

Sparrowhawk

Size: 28–38 cm
Latin name: Accipiter nisus
Family: Hawks, vultures and eagles
Habitat: Woodland and towns and cities
Food: Small birds
Life span: Up to 10 years

Thin legs

Sparrowhawks are birds of prey. Males have a grey back and white underparts; females (pictured) and their young are larger, with brown upperparts and lighter underparts. They have bars across their chest. They like to hunt for small birds in small spaces, so you might see them in your garden. In cold weather they will visit gardens to try and snatch a bird from a bird table. They fly quickly and do not hover like Kestrels.

Red Kite

Size: 60–66 cm
Latin name: *Milvus milvus*
Family: Hawks, vultures and eagles
Habitat: Fields, woodland and moorland
Food: Carrion, worms and occasionally small mammals
Life span: Up to 25 years

White patches
under wings

Red Kites
have a wing
span of nearly
two metres!

This large bird of prey
has a reddish-brown body
and a fan-shaped tail. It was saved
from extinction and is now common
across central England and central Scotland.

Dark blue cap →

Swallow

Size: 17–19 cm
Latin name: *Hirundo rustica*
Family: Swallows and martins
Habitat: Open fields, near water and farm buildings
Food: Insects
Life span: Up to 5 years

← Dark blue back

Swallows are small birds, distinctive for their forked tail. They have a dark blue back, a rust-red throat and pale underparts. Swallows only visit Britain in the summer. They can often be seen flying low over water.

House Martin

Size: 12 cm
Latin name: *Delichon urbica*
Family: Swallows and martins
Habitat: Towns and cities, farmland and woodland
Food: Insects
Life span: Up to 5 years

White rump

A House Martin's legs and toes are covered in white feathers.

House Martins are smaller than Swallows, with a shorter forked tail. They have bluey-black upperparts, white underparts and a distinctive white rump. They build mud nests under the eaves of buildings.

Swift

Size: 16–17 cm
Latin name: *Apus apus*
Family: Swifts
Habitat: Towns and cities, farmland and woodland
Food: Insects
Life span: Up to 10 years

Swifts feed, mate and even sleep while in the air. They may spend three years in flight without landing once.

Forked tail

The Swift has curved wings that look crescent-shaped in flight. They fly up very high, landing only to breed. Swifts are dark blackish-brown with a pale throat and face and a short forked tail.

Fieldfare

Size: 25 cm
Latin name: *Turdus pilaris*
Family: Chats and thrushes
Habitat: Countryside, hedges and trees
Food: Insects, worms and berries
Life span: 5–10 years

The Fieldfare looks very similar to a Mistle Thrush, but the markings on its chest are more defined and 'v'-shaped. Its wings are darker, too, and it has a yellowish throat and bill. Fieldfares are often seen in large flocks, especially in winter. They come to Britain from Scandinavia from October until May.

Redwing

Size: 21 cm
Latin name: *Turdus iliacus*
Family: Chats and thrushes
Habitat: Farmland, parks and countryside
Food: Insects, nuts and seeds
Life span: Up to 5 years

Redwings look very similar to Thrushes, but they have a distinctive orange-red patch beneath their wings and a yellowy stripe over their eyes. They arrive in October and leave again in the spring.

Watch out for flocks feeding on berries.

Tree Sparrow

Size: 14 cm
Latin name: *Passer montanus*
Family: Sparrows
Habitat: Uplands, woodland and hedgerows
Food: Seeds and insects
Life span: 2—5 years

The Tree Sparrow is similar to a House Sparrow, but less common and a bit smaller. It has a reddish-brown cap and white cheeks with a black spot.

Nuthatch

Size: 14 cm
Latin name: *Sitta europaea*
Family: Nuthatches
Habitat: Woodland and parks
Food: Insects, nuts and seeds
Life span: 2—3 years

The Nuthatch has a very striking orange-brown chest with blue-grey upperparts and a long black bill. Look for them on the side of tree trunks and the underside of branches.

Nuthatches can walk upside down on trees.

Kingfisher

Size: 16–17 cm
Latin name: *Alcedo atthis*
Family: Kingfishers
Habitat: Rivers and lakes
Food: Fish and insects
Life span: 5–10 years

Kingfishers lay their glossy white eggs at the end of burrows in riverbanks.

Long pointed bill

Kingfishers will fly past you quickly in a flash of shiny blue and bright orange. They may, very occasionally, visit garden ponds. Usually, they can be found sat at the edge of rivers as they hunt for fish.

Black-headed Gull

Size: 34–37 cm
Latin name: *Chroicocephalus ridibundus*
Family: Gulls
Habitat: Inland as well as coastal
Food: Worms, insects, fish and carrion
Life span: 10–15 years

Black-headed Gulls are the most common inland gulls in the UK.

The Black-headed Gull is found inland as well as by the coast. In the summer, it has a distinctive black head (main picture), but for the rest of the year it has a white head with chocolate brown stripes (top picture). These gulls are usually seen in small groups or flocks.

Herring Gull

Size: 55–67 cm
Latin name: *Larus argentatus*
Family: Gulls
Habitat: Coasts, fields, reservoirs and lakes
Food: Fish and scraps
Life span: 10–20 years

The Herring Gull is the most commonly seen gull by the coast. It is a large, noisy gull with a light grey back and white underparts. It has a hooked bill marked with a red spot. The red spot on a Herring Gull's bill is a target for its hungry chicks. When they peck this spot, the adult opens its bill and releases food into the mouths of the young gulls.

Common Gull

Size: 55–60 cm
Latin name: *Larus canus*
Family: Gulls
Habitat: Coasts, marshes, towns and parks
Food: Fish, carrion and insects
Life span: Up to 10 years

The Common Gull looks very similar to a Herring Gull, with grey wings, a black tail with white bars, a white head and body, and a yellow bill. In winter (pictured) their white head gets grey specks. They are often seen in towns, parks and playing fields in winter.

Mute Swan

Size: 140–160 cm
Latin name: *Cygnus olor*
Family: Swans, ducks and geese
Habitat: Rivers, ponds and lakes
Food: Water plants, insects and snails
Life span: 15–20 years

Young swans are called cygnets.

Mute Swans are Britain's largest bird. They are white with a long 's'-shaped neck and an orange bill with a black tip. They have a lump at the top of their bill. Swans can get angry and will hiss and flap their wings. A male swan is called a 'cob'; a female is called a 'pen'.

Canada Goose

Size: 90–110 cm
Latin name: *Branta canadensis*
Family: Swans, ducks and geese
Habitat: Rivers, ponds and lakes
Food: Roots, grass, leaves and seeds
Life span: 20–25 years

Canada Geese were introduced to Britain from North America.

Gosling

Canada Geese have a long black
neck and a black head with a white throat.
Their body is brown and they have black webbed
feet. You can often see large numbers of noisy Canada
Geese forming flocks together in parks and on open land.
Groups fly in a 'v'-shaped formation.

Greylag Goose

Size: 75–90 cm
Latin name: *Anser anser*
Family: Swans, ducks and geese
Habitat: Rivers, ponds and lakes
Food: Roots, grass and cereal
Life span: 15–20 years

The Greylag Goose is greyish-brown with a white patch under its tail. It has an orange bill, pink legs and webbed feet. These geese can be found in flocks on or beside water, or grazing on farmland. They are noisy birds.

Mallard

Size: 50–65 cm
Latin name: *Anas platyrhynchos*
Family: Swans, ducks and geese
Habitat: Ponds, rivers and lakes
Food: Seeds, acorns and berries,
plants, insects and shellfish.
Life span: 15–25 years

Mallards have a clutch of 9–13 eggs.

Female

Male

The Mallard is the most
common type of duck in Britain.
The male Mallard has a green head,
a white ring around its neck, a brown
breast and a pale grey back. The female
Mallard is speckled brown.

Tufted Duck

Size: 40–47 cm
Latin name: *Aythya fuligula*
Family: Swans, ducks and geese
Habitat: Ponds, lakes and reservoirs
Food: Molluscs, insects and plants
Life span: 10–15 years

Female Tufted Duck

Male Tufted Duck

This common duck is easy to identify by the tuft on the back of its head. The male is a glossy black and white and the female is dark brown. They can often been seen diving for food.

Pochard

Size: 42–49 cm
Latin name: *Aythya ferina*
Family: Swans, ducks and geese
Habitat: Ponds, lakes and reservoirs
Food: Plants and seeds, snails,
small fish and insects
Life span: 8–10 years

Pochards make nests in hollows in the ground. They nest separately, but will form large flocks in the winter.

The Pochard is smaller
than a Mallard. The male is
very recognisable with a red head and
neck and a black breast and tail (pictured).
The female is brown with a dark head and
blotchy cheeks. They dive for food.

Moorhen

Size: 32–35 cm
Latin name: *Gallinula chloropus*
Family: Swans, ducks and geese
Habitat: Ponds, rivers and lakes
Food: Water plants, seeds, fruit, grasses, insects, snails, worms and small fish
Life span: up to 15 years

Moorhens are black, with a red forehead and a yellow-tipped red bill. They have long green toes and white along their wings and tail.

Coot

Size: 36 38 cm
Latin name: *Fulica atra*
Family: Rails
Habitat: Ponds, rivers and lakes
Food: Vegetation, snails and insect larvae
Life span: Up to 15 years

Coots and Moorhens can often be seen together, but Coots are slightly larger and have a white forehead and bill.

Coots can run along the surface of water.

Black tufts

Chick

Great Crested Grebe

Size: 46–51 cm
Latin name: *Podiceps cristatus*
Family: Grebes
Habitat: Ponds, lakes and rivers
Food: Fish
Life span: 10–15 years

In winter, Great Crested Grebes are white underneath and brown above. But in summer, they have magnificent head tufts and chestnut brown cheek ruffs (pictured). Grebes dive often for food, and have a very long pointed bill.

Little Grebe

Size: 25–29 cm
Latin name: *Tachybaptus ruficollis*
Family: Grebes
Habitat: Ponds, lakes and rivers
Food: Insects, larvae and small fish

Little Grebes are brown with reddish cheeks in summer (pictured) and are much paler in winter. They are round-shaped and have fluffy white bottoms. The Little Grebe has a sharp pointed bill. It likes to dive in the water and can be quite a noisy bird.

Little Grebes nest on floating waterweed.

Grey Heron

Size: 90–98 cm
Latin name: *Ardea cinerea*
Family: Bitterns and herons
Habitat: Ponds, lakes and rivers
Food: Fish, small mammals and amphibians
Life span: Up to 25 years

Black spots

Grey Herons can sometimes be mistaken for birds of prey, because they circle high up in the sky.

Grey Herons are tall grey birds with a white head and a long yellow beak. They have a black streak on top of their head that ends in a tuft. Grey Herons stand tall and very still for a long time.

Cormorant

Size: 80–100 cm
Latin name: *Phalacrocorax carbo*
Family: Cormorants and shags
Habitat: Rivers, ponds and lakes
Food: Fish
Life span: 15–20 years

The Cormorant has a long neck and a hooked bill. They can often been seen with their wings stretched out, sat low down by the water.

Shag

Size: 65–80 cm
Latin name: *Phalacrocorax aristotelis*
Family: Cormorants and shags
Habitat: Coasts and lakes
Food: Fish and sometimes molluscs
Life span: Up to 15 years

Smaller and slimmer than Cormorants, the Shag has a small crest on its forehead. Its neck also has more of an 's' shape.

In spring, Shags grow dark green feathers.

Puffin

Size: 26–29 cm
Latin name: *Fratercula arctica*
Family: Auks
Habitat: Coasts
Food: Fish
Life span: 10–20 years

The small silver fish in the Puffin's mouth are called sand eels. They are the Puffin's favourite food. Puffins can't live without them.

These birds are very recognisable by their coloured, curved beak. They have white cheeks and white underparts with a black back and bright orange legs. They nest in colonies on cliffs.

How to attract birds to your garden

In recent years, many familiar birds, such as Starlings, House Sparrows and Song Thrushes, have started to disappear from UK gardens. You can help increase their numbers by putting different types of food out and by looking after your garden.

Food for all your favourite birds

Birds need food with lots of fat in it to help them survive cold weather. Make them fat balls with lard or beef suet. Fat from cooking is bad for birds, as are polyunsaturated margarines and vegetable oils.

Seeds will attract Sparrows, Dunnocks, finches and Collared Doves. Blackbirds love flaked maize and sultanas. Goldfinches and Siskins love sunflower seeds. Peanuts are popular with many types of birds, including tits, Greenfinches, House Sparrows, Great Spotted Woodpeckers and Siskins. Crushed or grated nuts are great for Robins, Dunnocks and Wrens. Do not use salted or dry roasted peanuts. Some birds, such as Blackbirds, will take fresh meaty dog or cat food.

Make your own bird feeder

1 Use a pencil to make a hole in the bottom of a yogurt pot. Ask an adult to help.

2 Tie a length of string to a lollypop stick and thread the other end through the yogurt pot hole.

3 Mix together some oats, raisins, breadcrumbs, unsalted peanuts, stale cake crumbs or sunflower seeds. You can choose what to mix together.

4 Add an equal amount of chopped squares of lard to the mixture. Squeeze it with your fingers to make a ball of lard and nut mix.

5 Spoon the lard mixture into the yogurt pot. Leave in the fridge for an hour to harden.

6 Once it is set, slide the yogurt pot off and hang your bird feeder from a tree.

Watch birds come and visit.

Put out food and water twice daily in very cold and icy weather.

Further information

Places to visit

Wildfowl & Wetlands Trust

Slimbridge
Gloucestershire
GL2 7BT
www.wwt.org.uk
The Wildfowl & Wetlands Trust (WWT) is one of the world's largest and most respected wetland conservation organisations. You can have a great day out visiting their wetland trusts in Castle Espie, County Down, Northern Ireland; Caerlaverock, Dunfriesshire; Washington, Tyne and Wear; Martin Mere, Lancashire; Welney in Norfolk; Slimbridge in Gloucestershire; Llanelli, Camarthenshire or Arundel, West Sussex.

RSPB Wildlife Explorer

The Lodge
Sandy
Beds SG19 2DL
You can visit The Lodge or go to:

www.rspb.org.uk/reserves/index.aspx to find more than 150 RSPB nature reserves where you can watch wildlife.

www.wildlifetrusts.org/reserves-wildlife
Go to this website to find a nature reserve near you.

Useful websites

www.rspb.org.uk
A fantastic website with information on every bird, including a bird identifier. Learn how to register for the Big Garden Birdwatch.

www.garden-birds.co.uk
A very thorough resource. Provides a handy A–Z of British birds with pictures and silhouettes of birds in flight, song recordings and information on nests and chicks.

www.birdingforall.com
Birding For All is an organisation seeking to improve access for people with disabilities to reserves, facilities and services for birding.

www.bto.org/about-birds
They have a bird of the month and information on National Nest Box Week.

Useful books

British Animals: Owl by Stephen Savage (Wayland, 2010)

Coastal and Sea Birds Handbook by Duncan Brewor and Alan Harris (Miles Kelly, 2003)

I Spy Birds (Michelin, 2009)

RSPB Handbook of British Birds by Peter Holden and Tim Cleeves (Christopher Helm Publishers, 2008)

Usborne Spotter's Guides: Birds by Peter Holden (Usborne, 2006)

How many different birds can you spot in your local area?

Glossary

amphibian animals with cold blood that live in the water when young but move onto the land as adults

bar a patch of colour

beak the hard mouth part of a bird

belly the part of a bird's body between its breast and its tail

bird of prey a bird which hunts other animals or birds for food

breast the part of a bird's body between its throat and belly

carrion the flesh of dead animals

clutch a group of eggs laid at one time

colonies groups of birds that live together

crest a tuft of feathers on a bird's head

crown the top part of a bird's head

eaves the space between the walls and the roof of a building

extinct none of the species are alive any more

family a grouping of species that are similar

flock a group of birds

forage to search for food on the ground

game birds that are hunted by humans for sport and for food

habitat the place where a species of bird or animal lives

hover when a bird stays in one place in the air by flapping its wings very fast

inland a part of the country that is not near the sea

mate when a male and female come together to produce young

migrate when birds move from one place to another, usually to find food or because of climate

nocturnal active at night

plumage a bird's feathers

predator an animal that hunts and kills other animals or birds for food

prey an animal hunted and eaten by another animal

roost a place where birds rest together, often in a group

rump the area of a bird's body above its tail

sheen a gloss or shine on a surface

species a group of birds that all look alike and behave in the same way

streaks long or narrow marks

talon the claw of a bird of prey

underparts the lower part of a bird's body

upperparts the upper part of a bird's body

wattle a fold of skin dangling from a bird's head or throat

Learn the different parts of a bird's body for easier identification.

Index